MARSHALL FIELD'S

A BUILDING BOOK FROM
THE CHICAGO
ARCHITECTURE FOUNDATION

JAY PRIDMORE

Pomegranate

SAN FRANCISCO

Published by Pomegranate Communications, Inc.

Box 808022, Petaluma, CA 94975

800 277 1428; www.pomegranate.com

Pomegranate Europe Ltd.

Unit 1, Heathcote Business Centre, Hurlbutt Road

Warwick, Warwickshire CV34 6TD, UK

[+44] 0 1926 430111; sales@pomeurope.co.uk

Library of Congress Cataloging-in-Publication Data

Pridmore, Jay,

    Marshall Field's : a building book from the Chicago Architecture Foundation/Jay Pridmore.

       p. cm.

    ISBN 978-0-7649-2018-9 (alk. paper)

      1. Marshall Field's (Department store) 2. Architecture—Illinois—Chicago—19th
century. 3. Eclecticism in architecture—Illinois—Chicago. 4. Burnham, Daniel Hudson,
1846–1912. 5. Chicago (Ill.)—Buildings, structures, etc. I. Marshall Field's (Department
store) II. Chicago Architecture Foundation. III. Title.

NA6227.D45 P75 2002

720'.92'2—dc21

                                   2001054882

Pomegranate Catalog No. A624

Cover and book design by Lynn Bell, Monroe Street Studios, Santa Rosa, CA

Printed in Korea

14 13 12 11 10 09 08 07 06   11 10 9 8 7 6 5 4 3

M ı s s ı o n

The Chicago Architecture Foundation
(CAF) is dedicated to advancing public
interest and education in architecture and
related design. CAF pursues this mission
through a comprehensive program of
tours, lectures, exhibitions, special pro-
grams, and youth programs, all designed to enhance the public's awareness
and appreciation of Chicago's outstanding architectural legacy.

Founded in 1966, the Chicago Architecture Foundation has evolved to
become a nationally recognized resource advancing public interest and
education in Chicago's outstanding architecture. Its programs serve more than
250,000 people each year. For more information contact us at the address
below, or visit us on our website:

Chicago Architecture Foundation

224 South Michigan Avenue

Chicago IL 60604

312-922-TOUR (8687)

www.architecture.org

TIMELINE OF CONSTRUCTION

1852   Marshall Field & Co.'s predecessor, P. Palmer & Co., opens in a storefront in Chicago on Lake Street near Clark Street.

1858   P. Palmer & Co. moves to more spacious quarters on Lake Street; the building has a classical facade and large store windows.

1865   Potter Palmer takes on two young partners, Levi Leiter and Marshall Field.

1868   Field, Palmer & Leiter move their store to a large "marble palace," designed by John Van Osdel, at State and Washington Streets. This building will burn in the Great Chicago Fire of 1871.

1873   A new store, now called Field, Leiter & Co., is built at State and Washington Streets in the French Second Empire style. It is known as the Singer Building because it is owned by the Singer Sewing Machine Company. It will burn to the ground in 1877.

1879   The second Singer Building is built on the site of the former and occupied by the Field, Leiter & Co. Designed by architect E. S. Jennison, this will remain the main building of the growing Marshall Field & Co. (as the store is renamed in 1881) until it is razed in 1906.

1893 The Marshall Field Annex is built at the corner of Washington
      Street and Wabash Avenue in Florentine Renaissance style. The
      architect is D. H. Burnham & Co.

1902 The North State section of Marshall Field & Co. is completed at
      State and Randolph Streets, in the commercial Beaux-Arts style,
      designed by Daniel Burnham's firm. This style will be used in each
      successive addition to the State Street Store.

1906 The Middle Wabash section goes up on Wabash Avenue, mid-
      block between Washington and Randolph Streets.

1907 Marshall Field's South State section, with the great dome by Louis
      Comfort Tiffany, replaces the second Singer Building at State and
      Washington Streets.

1914 North Wabash is completed. This final section on the store's full
      city block includes the Narcissus Room on the seventh floor.

1914 Marshall Field & Co. Store for Men, otherwise known as the Annex,
      is completed across Washington Street from the first Annex.
      Designed by Graham, Anderson, Probst and White, successor firm
      to D. H. Burnham & Co., the twenty-story building combines
      Marshall Field's need for more retail space in the first six stories
      with profitable rental offices in the remaining fourteen floors.

INTRODUCTION

Just a few years before the architect Daniel H. Burnham, who authored the 1909 Plan of Chicago, uttered the unforgettable words, "Make no little plans," his client Marshall Field I was building the largest department store in the world. Field had already created the most successful wholesale dry goods business in existence and was keenly involved in other businesses, making Chicago both the rail hub of the nation and the financial center of America's westward expansion.

Because of these activities, Marshall Field was considered the richest man in a city famous for phenomenally rich men. He was also a builder known best for what is now called Marshall Field's State Street Store. From the time it became State Street's centerpiece, the store was Chicago's great retail palace. Then as now, this store did more than house a great merchant's business; it would stand as a lasting monument to Marshall Field's protean enterprise.

Today, Marshall Field's is a different store from the emporium of the past, when it was known everywhere for unexcelled grandeur and luxury. What has not changed is the splendor of its architecture, a building that continues to inspire awe and sustain the reputation of Marshall Field's as one of the truly great department stores of the world.

Perhaps Field had posterity in mind when he began to imagine the State Street complex. Or perhaps he simply had the presence of mind to commission architects sure to accomplish the complex task before them. Indeed, the building

Young Marshall Field had been a shopkeeper in western Massachusetts when he arrived in Chicago in 1856. Nine years later, at the age of thirty, he was a partner in Field, Palmer & Leiter Co. dry goods. Shown here in his forties, Field had already acquired immense power. When he died in 1906, he was regarded as the leading merchant in America and very likely the world.

had many requirements, one of which was to make an architectural statement in a city already noted for its architecture. Another need was efficient interiors in order to sell merchandise on a scale then unknown in the dry goods business. Perhaps most importantly, Field set his sights on creating a place where the public—he never lost sight of his customers—would be dazzled by opulence.

Daniel Burnham and other architects who worked for Field fulfilled these requirements. When the most lavish section of the State Street Store, called South State, opened in 1907, the hundreds of thousands who came just to witness touches of storybook elegance—including a favrile glass mosaic dome six stories above the main sales floor—stared in jaw-dropping admiration. The central aisle of the store resembled the "many pillared hall of the Madura temple in South India," wrote a professor of art at the University of Chicago. The dome, executed by the workshop of Louis Comfort Tiffany, was "one step forward in realization of William Morris's prediction that 'One day we shall win back art for the people.'"

Despite elements of fantasy, Marshall Field & Co. was also very much in tune with the realities of the time. Both Field and Burnham were capitalists par excellence who understood the social and business conditions that made Chicago the fastest-growing city in the world. Not only were new industries creating new prosperity—steel mills, grain exchanges, and stockyards—but new means of transportation were now able to deliver an unbelievable range of merchandise from the far corners of the world.

View of the State Street Store from the corner of Randolph Street. This
is a place for everyone. Its architecture has touches of Beaux-Arts and
the Chicago School, and its facade dominates Chicago's most popular
thoroughfare with a magnificence that invites the public inside.

Fortunately, Field and Burnham made the most of the opportunity. The merchant and the architect incorporated both the inspirational and the practical—so often the ingredients of architectural icons—and created a place that has outlived a succession of fashions in dry goods and retailing. Many times since it opened, Marshall Field's State Street Store has adjusted to modern times and reinvented itself. But each alteration has been enriched with an architectural setting that has not changed, in a place that is as timeless as a commercial building can be.

The Advent of State Street

The store that would become Marshall Field & Co. had its beginnings in 1852. Called P. Palmer & Co. after founder Potter Palmer, a recent arrival from New York State, it was not initially a store of great distinction; Palmer's line of dry goods, including fabric, hosiery, gloves, and brocades, was not too different from that of the competition. If anything distinguished P. Palmer & Co., it was the proprietor's generous use of display windows, rarely seen on mud-spattered Lake Street at the time. Palmer took special care to array fine scarves and handsome gowns against delicate backdrops of lace and white crepe. Chicago was still a rough hewn frontier outpost, but its growing population of women, hungry for touches of refinement, responded and became Palmer's loyal customers.

Photograph © Hedrich Blessing

The early twentieth century was a moment when skyscrapers were ascendant and dramatic interiors de rigueur in grand department stores. Marshall Field's State Steet Store, especially the North State atrium, was the beneficiary of this marriage of two strong architectural trends.

In 1858 Palmer set himself apart again by moving to new quarters on Lake Street. Now "one of the finest and most costly business blocks in the United States," as the *Tribune* reported, the store was Italianate on the outside and inside included "a gem of an apartment which the fair shopper will readily appreciate as a shawl and mantilla room."

Chicago continued to be a city of sharp contrasts, including the harsh difference between Palmer's tasteful selling floors and the indignities of Lake Street, still a quagmire reputed to swallow horses and wagons in one gulp. Palmer's next move, therefore, was not just to expand and improve his own dry goods store but to go much further and transform Chicago's shopping district at large.

To effect such change, Palmer began by forming a partnership with two young and talented retail men: Levi Leiter, who had come to Chicago from Maryland, and Marshall Field, a native of western Massachusetts. Beginning in 1865, Leiter and Field minded the store—now named Field, Palmer & Leiter— while Palmer acquired property along State Street, which he now envisioned as Chicago's next great shopping district.

Within a year or so, Palmer left the retail business altogether to concentrate on real estate, first widening State Street and then lining it with stylish buildings. The first building, completed in 1868, was for rental to the dry goods establishment now called Field, Leiter & Co. This six-story "marble palace" at State and Washington Streets was designed by Chicago's first trained architect,

Lake Street between Clark and Dearborn Streets was the commercial nexus of Chicago when the city was a frontier "metropolis." In the five-story storefront mid-block, Potter Palmer's dry goods store was one of the biggest retail establishments among many. It was also the most refined at a time when refinement was very rare indeed in this—and any other—neighborhood in Chicago.

John Van Osdel, in the Second Empire style, the result, no doubt, of Palmer's recent trip to Paris. That city was just then in the throes of a massive redesign by Napoleon II and his master builder, Baron George von Haussmann.

Imperial distinction was fleeting, however, as the store disintegrated with the rest of State Street, including the first Palmer House Hotel, in the Great Chicago Fire that began the evening of October 8, 1871. For a few hours that night, there was hope for the store, or at least time for a legion of Field and Leiter employees, who arrived before dawn, to stoke the boilers, run the elevators, and save some inventory. But the flames quickly reached the Loop, and before sunset the next day the marble palace, so-called for the Connecticut white marble of its facade, had crumbled with some $2 million of merchandise inside.

The Singer Building

Field, Leiter & Co. recovered quicker than anyone believed possible. A week after the fire, they were in temporary quarters in a horsecar barn south of the Loop. In 1873 they were back at their former site on State Street, in new quarters called the Singer Building, named after the Singer Sewing Machine Company, which built, owned, and rented it to Field and Leiter. The store's new French-style home resembled their old one, although this one included several features that greatly enhanced its function. It had a large central atrium, for example, covered by a glass skylight that filled all six floors with precious natural light. This style foreshadowed the emerging Chicago School, as did the Singer Building's understated use of limestone instead of flashy marble.

The Great Chicago Fire of 1871 devastated Field, Leiter & Co but did not alter its destiny. This photograph shows the extent of the devastation; it also reveals that the first State Street store was undergirded with iron supports and columns, devices that speeded construction and foreshadowed the type of commercial building that would distinguish the Chicago School of architecture, which prevailed by the late 1880s.

Field, Leiter & Co. set a sophisticated tone for the architecture of State Street when the store's first "marble palace" (above) was built in 1868 by developer Potter Palmer and architect John Van Osdel. It was destroyed in the Great Chicago Fire of 1871 and replaced by another French-style emporium (right) completed in 1873. This one was called the Singer Building as it was owned by the sewing machine company of the same name and rented to the store that made State Street a great street. Another fire took the Singer Building in 1877, and it was replaced yet again in the style of Chicago's frontier version of a Second Empire palais.

The Second Singer Building

Another fire took the Singer Building in 1877, and once again Field and Leiter recovered quickly, first moving to quarters in the Inter-State Exposition Building, an iron-and-glass hall partially inspired by London's Crystal Palace. The Exposition Building offered excellent space and light, but its location, on the site of today's Art Institute, was too far off the beaten track. Thus, Field, Leiter & Co. moved into its third State Street store in 1879, again at State and Washington Streets and again rented from the Singer Company. Stylistically described as "French Renaissance," the second Singer Building had additional new interior features: "imposing columns of ornate design, beautiful railings, and bracketed cornices," as one newspaper reported. These elements reflected the Art Nouveau movement, then evolving in France and America, in which the structural elements of buildings often provided the potential for dazzling decoration.

The Marshall Field Wholesale Store

The second Singer Building, razed in 1906, was remembered for years as a building of exquisite taste and luxury. It was not Marshall Field's most important piece of bygone architecture, however; that honor went to the Marshall Field Wholesale Store, built in 1887 on a full city block at Adams and Franklin Streets. This structure housed another, vastly larger segment of Marshall Field & Co., as the company was renamed after Field and Leiter ended their partnership in 1881.

By 1879, a third State Street Store went up on State and Washington Streets, modeled largely after previous versions. Called the "second Singer Building," it featured an extravagant roofline—arguably more beautiful than previous versions—and an interior with cornices, railings, and metalwork inspired by Art Nouveau, the style recently imported from France. In Chicago, where builders were seeking to combine the beauty of elaborate form with the needs of practical function, this building was a feast for both architects and consumers.

Field's wholesale division was created to supply merchandise to dry goods and general stores throughout the American West, which was just then burgeoning with the explosive expansion of the railroads. As Chicago was the rail hub of the West, and as Marshall Field was Chicago's leading merchant, this side of the business brought in immense wealth. Thus, when the wholesale division needed more space, Field naturally hired one of the leading architects in the United States, Henry Hobson Richardson, to design it.

Richardson could be depended upon to design something powerful. For some years he had been developing a distinctly American style, rejecting neoclassical and other European prototypes popular at the time, instead creating a style that became known as "Richardsonian Romanesque." This design typically featured heavy stone walls and powerful arches that reflected, Richardson believed, the simple integrity and unshakable strength that symbolized America.

Richardson's model for the Wholesale Store undoubtedly was Palazzo Pitti in Florence, one of the simplest but most imposing buildings of the Italian Renaissance. Pitti's massive walls and great arches clearly inspired Richardson, as did the Medici family who occupied it and whose immense wealth and power seemed, Richardson noted, to foreshadow Field's.

The Wholesale Store was more than an imitation, however. Its design blended other architectural influences, such as the proportions and oversized

By 1897, when this photograph was taken, ornate metalwork and elaborate display windows made State Street an exciting, stimulating, and prosperous street. In the background are horse-drawn buses, which Field's provided to carry customers from the railway stations to the store and then back again when they had finished shopping.

The main building of Marshall Field & Co. in the 1890s had a thoroughly modern interior, with iron columns, glass-enclosed atrium, and abundant natural light. It reflected a new social order, as the department store became a public stage for social interaction and the purchase of household necessities.

windows of a New England industrial mill.
Partly, Richardson was celebrating
Marshall Field's Yankee roots, but this
choice was also practical. Just as natural
light was a necessity in old factories, it was
beneficial here, where buyers came to
inspect wholesale merchandise up close
and place orders for their stores at home.

Richardson accomplished all he set out to do with such originality and elegance that Louis Sullivan, perhaps Chicago's greatest architect of the period and
certainly its most mellifluous, called the Wholesale Store "a monument to trade,
to the organized commercial spirit, to the power and progress of the age." The
Wholesale Store was torn down in 1930, but during its lifetime, Richardson's
building set an architectural tone and standard that Marshall Field, his successors, and their architects were consciously determined to uphold.

Palazzo on Wabash Avenue

By the early 1890s, Marshall Field & Co. was ready to enlarge its retail space
and chose the northwest corner of Washington Street and Wabash Avenue for
what would be called "The Annex." By now, building styles had changed from the
Singer Building next door. Chicago architecture was making its mark primarily
through a number of local architects, later known as the Chicago School.

Beginning in the 1880s, these architects were achieving a national reputation for simple but refined buildings, such as the Monadnock by John Wellborn Root and the Auditorium by Adler & Sullivan. These buildings were praised with words ranging from "ferocious" to "sublime."

In this architectural setting, Field gave The Annex commission to Daniel H. Burnham, one of the city's leading architects at the time. If this had happened just a few years earlier, Field might have had a much different building, since Burnham and particularly his late partner John Root had been leading adherents of the Chicago School. But Root died in 1891, and Burnham was now seeking to transform urban architecture, primarily in his new role as director of architecture for the 1893 World's Columbian Exposition. Burnham's ambition—and that of the captains of Chicago industry who hired him—was to create a White City of neoclassical palaces, splendid enough to make Chicago "Paris on the Prairie," as it was being called, or "Athens on the Lake." To achieve such a transformation, Burnham hired architects primarily from the East who could be counted on to build Chicago's Fair in a Beaux-Arts style in tune with the prestige some Chicagoans believed they deserved.

When Marshall Field commissioned Burnham to build The Annex, it was with the understanding that the new store would open about the same time as the Exposition and in many ways echo it. Thus, Marshall Field's next building represented a partial renunciation of Chicago's recent architectural past. It would be a mistake, however, to say that the Chicago School left

The Marshall Field Wholesale Store,
designed by H. H. Richardson and
completed in 1887, was—and is—
regarded as a major turning point in
urban American architecture. Although
razed in 1930s, its strength, character,
and functionality set the standard for
the architecture of Marshall Field & Co.
for years to come.

Marshall Field's Annex of 1893, at the corner of Washington Street and Wabash Avenue, was the work of architect Daniel Burnham and his firm's principal designer, Charles Atwood. Atwood designed the Palace of Fine Arts—rebuilt to be the Museum of Science and Industry—at the World's Columbian Exposition about the same time.

without a trace. In fact, the rectilinear Annex is one of Chicago's best blends of the fashionable Beaux-Arts and the more ferocious Chicago School.

Again Burnham looked to Florence for inspiration. On the outside The Annex borrows details from many early Renaissance palazzi, themselves inspired by classical form and structural clarity. Like many palazzi of the fifteenth century, The Annex is luxurious and noble, but it also reveals a sense of structure and function. Its rusticated base has heavy arches with elaborate stonework, decorative to be sure but also framing large display windows. The building rises ten stories in height, dissolving gracefully into lighter ornament and smaller windows in the rental offices on the fifth through tenth floors.

The Annex became popular with shoppers and office tenants alike. Sadly, the avant-garde of Chicago architecture despaired of it. Louis Sullivan, bitter about the eclipse of Chicago's original architecture, wrote that The Annex was "not characteristic of the West. . . . It lacks, utterly, Western frankness, direct-ness, crudity, if you will. It is merely a weak-rooted cutting from an Eastern hothouse: and it languishes in the open air."

But the Exposition, and in many ways the Marshall Field Annex, served as models for the neoclassical trend in commercial architecture that was then in

Linens were one of the oldest and most honored departments of any dry goods establishment, and Marshall Field & Co. operated an extensive one in The Annex. This business was large enough to be divided between the main selling space on the second floor (facing page) and the Art Linen Room nearby, where the finest goods were quietly sold.

In 1893, the Tea Room at Marshall Field's filled the entire fourth floor of The Annex. Only a few years before, Field had reluctantly permitted rudimentary food service in the store. By now the restaurants were becoming a Chicago institution, as were menu items such as corned beef hash and chicken pot pie.

The urban aesthetic in the early 1900s was to find form and
function in metal. Marshall Field's architects deftly achieved
this goal in this canopy over the door on Washington Street.

progress. Daniel Burnham led his profession nationwide during this period precisely because of his ability to combine many influences and needs, creating buildings that expressed a philosophical spirit, functioned usefully, and for those reasons became enduring architectural monuments.

The World's Largest Retail Establishment

By the turn of the century, as Chicago became one of the world's fastest-growing cities, State Street assumed its role as a great commercial thoroughfare, lined with stores, shoppers, and a splendor that might have seemed preposterous just a generation before. During the first decade of the new century, seven major stores were attracting clients to State Street, all inspired by the success of Marshall Field & Co.

Field's maintained its lead by defining quality goods and the manner of selling them. John G. Shedd, who became president of the store after Marshall Field's death in 1906, reasoned that if higher-grade goods were given an air of privacy and specialization, they would appeal more strongly to the preferred clientele. But increasing business under such circumstances also meant ever-growing space requirements, such that by the beginning of the new century, Field's needed to expand again.

The 1902 grand opening of the North State Street section of the store was a grand occasion for Marshall Field's "drapers," and it kept the shuttle from Northwestern Station busy. Decades later the store constructed an El station on the Wabash Avenue side—convenient but lacking the theatricality of a horse-drawn coach.

The thirteen-story North State section of Marshall Field's State Street Store, completed in 1902, epitomized the Chicago ideal that "form follows function." A great skylight admitted a flood of merchandise-enhancing natural light. The balcony became stage settings where Chicago women came to see and be seen.

The Marshall Field State Street Store was the subject of an infinite number of
postcards, including these images. The Library and Writing Room (above)
and the Silence Room (below) offered customers moments of repose.

A Splendid View

One of the two immense light shafts which go to make this store the best lighted and the best ventilated store in the world.

Marshall Field & Co.

Telephone "Private Exchange-One"
250 Branch Telephones Placed all Over the Store

Left: The marble, mosaics, and streams of light that filled the main entrance on State Street transmitted a sense of personal well being to customers as they crossed the teeming street to the refined precincts within. This illustration for a brochure explains why the public at large benefited from good modern architecture.

Opposite: Marshall Field's best-known icon—among many—is the Great Clock. The first one was mounted in the second Singer Building in 1897 when Marshall Field discovered that the corner of State and Washington Streets had become a meeting place, and notes were being pasted on the store's display windows. To encourage promptness—and discourage defacement of the windows—Field had a bronze clock erected in 1897. A new clock was cast in 1907 for the South State Street opening, and another one was later mounted at the opposite end at State and Randolph Streets. The clock appeared on a 1945 Norman Rockwell cover of *The Saturday Evening Post*.

One of the most enduring elements of Marshall Field's is the Walnut Room, two views of which are shown here. When the room, named after its Circassian walnut paneling, opened in 1907 in the South State Street section, it included the Tea Room (above), which was primarily for women, and the South Grill (facing page), designed more for men having lunch. Each year during the Christmas season the Walnut Room displayed a great tree.

The first phase of this expansion was completed in 1902, on the corner of State and Randolph Streets, where the so-called North State section of the State Street Store replaced Chicago's old Central Music Hall. The design for this thirteen-story addition—and for remaining sections that echoed it and eventually filled the entire city block—was the work of Peirce Anderson, Burnham's chief designer at this time, whose building differed markedly from the Florentine profile of The Annex. Anderson reflected Chicago's enduring commercial style—simple and understated—and conformed to the quiet horizontality that gave so many of Chicago's office buildings and even warehouses a kind of "architectural nobility," as one critic stated at the time.

Although the exterior of the State Street Store was simple, the interior emphatically was not. The most elaborate of the new sections, completed in 1907, replaced the 1879 Singer Building at State and Washington Streets with a sumptuousness that came to be synonymous with Marshall Field's. Its most notable feature, the great Tiffany dome, remains a stunning decorative feat. Composed of tens of thousands of glittering glass tesserae, the mosaic reflects the Art Nouveau ideal, shared by Louis Tiffany, that even the most lavish decoration must contribute integrally to function—both to define a great vaulted space and to unabashedly inspire the buying public.

Other now well-established elements of Marshall Field's were also new in 1907. Restaurants and food service were rare in dry goods establishments

Photograph © Hedrich Blessing

Artist Louis Comfort Tiffany enjoyed great success at the World's Columbian Exposition in 1893 and established a loyal and growing clientele in Chicago. The Marshall Field's dome, the largest of its kind in the world, represented a climax for his Chicago career, although other commissions followed, notably, the skylight in the Men's Grill of the Field's Annex at Washington Street and Wabash Avenue, which was built in 1914.

before Marshall Field's retail manager Harry Selfridge (later the founder of Selfridge's department store in London) insisted that shoppers would shop longer and buy more if they could stop for refreshment. Field was reluctant to take the dry goods business in that direction, but in 1890 he agreed to permit a small tearoom for ladies. The idea grew, and South State eventually included the Walnut Room, named for the Circassian walnut paneling, and several other restaurants eventually seating 2,800.

Completion

The final phase of the State Street Store's growth occurred in 1914 with the completion of the North Wabash section at Randolph Street and Wabash Avenue. This made Marshall Field's the world's largest department store and redefined department stores by offering an array of services unheard of in retail establishments of any type until that time. These services included a private transit station connected by a short bridge to the Wabash Avenue elevated. Services, mostly on the third floor, also included long-distance telephone, telegraph, stenographers, a travel agency, and even reading and writing rooms.

A Building for the Ages

In 1911, Marshall Field's State Street Store relinquished its title as the world's largest store, yielding to Wanamaker's of Philadelphia, also designed by Daniel Burnham & Co, and which Burnham called "the most notable of its kind that has

The great State Street Store permitted a much broader concept of customer services. In the 1920s, visitor services included a postal station, a theater ticket desk, long-distance telephone, stenographers, and a travel bureau. The service desk even provided a place for at least one customer to leave his ex-wife's alimony check.

After the thirteen-story North State Street section was completed in 1902, the Singer Building (on the right) was renovated. Its mansard roof came off, and street-level detailing was brought into line. Within five years, the old structure was razed, and the South State Street section went up, whereupon the Marshall Field State Street facade was as stately as its interiors were lavish.

In a store that had become so colorful and infused with Art Nouveau splendor, this 1923 cover of the Marshall Field's magazine, *Fashions of the Hour*, reflected the store's architecture while transmitting an unmistakable sense of style.

Completing the State Street Store in 1914 was the North Wabash section, where the Narcissus Room on the seventh floor demonstrated that classical interiors had not lost their appeal. The fountain was carved of Carrara marble, and it was topped with a bronze of the Roman god Narcissus. The room, now used for special events, remains one of many icons of the State Street Store.

Limousines pulled up to Marshall Field's all day during the flapper era. By 1925 it had become necessary to institute a parking service, as valets joined the doormen on the street to greet and cater to customers. Marshall Field's was well suited for Chicagoans partial to making a grand entrance.

even been undertaken by man." Burnham pointed out that Wanamaker's use of a Chicago architectural firm was not happenstance, implying that Chicago architects and Burnham in particular were the profession's experts at combining the functionality of a modern building with the prestige of classically inspired design. It followed that among department stores Marshall Field's was the first to demonstrate that, as another client stated, "the modern retail establishment is a very complicated machine for distributing merchandise."

Store for Men

For years thereafter, the Marshall Field State Street Store inspired other retail establishments and buildings in Chicago to architectural distinction. One such store was the Marshall Field's Store for Men, completed in 1914 across Washington Street from Burnham's 1893 Annex. The twenty-story Store for Men (confusingly sometimes called "The Annex") addressed a variety of demands, such as John Shedd's unexpurgated desire to eliminate cigar-smoking men from the refined precincts of the rest of the store and for first-class rental space in the office tower above the seventh floor.

This store, designed by Graham, Anderson, Probst and White, successor firm to D. H. Burnham & Co., had a different character from the State Street Store across the street but definitely came from the same family. The Store for Men was less decorative, more "masculine" and angular in design, yet its pillared sales floors and its Tiffany glass dome in the light well were unmistakable reminders of the luxury and loftiness that was Marshall Field's.

In 1914 the Store for Men was built across Washington Street from the 1893 Annex. Connected to the State Street Store by underground tunnel, the Store for Men building (also called "The Annex") separated the sometimes gruff male shoppers from the gentle sanctuary for which Marshall Field's was known. Nevertheless, the Store for Men contained all the imperial splendor that Field's architects, Graham, Anderson, Probst and White (successors to D. H. Burnham & Co.), could lavish on it, including the Men's Grill (above), with a glass-globe fountain beneath an elaborate domed skylight, both the work of the Louis Comfort Tiffany firm. Until it was dismantled in the 1970s, the grill was well suited for meetings: business could be discussed, and cigars could be smoked. The furnishings were in mahogany and leather; the red globe on the fountain symbolized the earth as a molten mass. The grill had a total seating capacity of 750, including seven party rooms and twenty-one booths.

The Merchandise Mart

Next in Marshall Field's monumental expansion was one of the most impressive buildings in Chicago's cityscape: the Merchandise Mart. Also designed by Graham, Anderson, Probst and White, the Mart was motivated by the company's sense of magnificence, in both form and function. The store's then-president, James Simpson, commissioned the Merchandise Mart in an effort to revive Field's flagging wholesale business; the building was completed in 1930. The effort was not successful—Field's wholesale slid to extinction, and the Mart was sold at a loss in 1945—but its enduring legacy is this building on the river, a great Art Moderne version of a Chicago-style loft.

The 28 Shop

One of the most elaborate changes in the retailing space of the State Street store occurred in 1941 with the opening of The 28 Shop, a new fashion salon dedicated to American designers, since World War II had ended the availability of European (primarily French) fashions. To make this area both elegant and exciting, the store engaged designer Joseph Platt, scenographer for *Gone with the Wind*, to create a sleek rotunda (appointed with Louis Quinze gilt and garlands) surrounded by large mirrored fitting rooms, each with a different design, ranging from stylish bamboo to the richness of Oriental rugs. The opening of The 28 Shop was the social event of the season, when Chicago's smart set arrived in limousines at the door at 28 East Washington Street and rode private elevators to the rarefied comforts of Chicago's most exclusive dress shop.

Photograph © Hedrich Blessing

The 28 Shop, established in 1941, brought a heightened sense of luxury to the couture department. Designed by Joseph Platt, set designer for some of Hollywood's biggest pictures, the sixth floor of the 1893 Annex was infused with the most modern theatricality. Its twenty-eight fitting rooms were decorated with lace valances, exotic bamboo furniture, or shocking pink upholstery. Tea was served on 28 Shop china, and customers could write notes on 28 Shop stationery.

The rectangular grid and open floor plan of the State Street Store, a classic element of Chicago commercial architecture, enabled maximum flexbility, such as the settings for ready-to-wear fashions, shown above and on the facing page, circa 1915.

Enormous strides in merchandising design were in the offing when display director Arthur Fraser joined Marshall Field's in 1895 and was given dictatorial control of window design. With the State Street Store's completion in 1914, Fraser's "canvas" was sixty-five large display windows. Fraser was a modernist who believed that abstract images were not only attractive but made visitors think and buy. By the early 1920s, Art Deco inspired streamlined surfaces and ziggurauts—with curvaceous fashions to complement the architecture (above). In 1931, a taste for the Viennese Secession movement generated designs of broad geometric shapes and rich surfaces (facing page). Other themes from Fraser's era, which ended in 1944, showed that he was never afraid of the elaborate or highly stylized image that left some conservative store executives shaking their heads.

In the following years, many other changes were made to the State Street Store; most attempted to uphold Marshall Field's delicate balance between sensation and dignity. In 1992, for example, a new atrium was built over what was Holden Court, the small utility street that separated the Wabash from the State Street sides of the store. The lustrous postmodern surfaces of this interior reflect the style in vogue at that time, yet the addition's most notable features vividly evoke the architectural standards of the past. Here, with banks of escalators soaring all through the thirteen-story space, a Field's retail space became a place to see and be seen in. Perhaps more sublime, a bronze fountain on the ground floor of this new atrium was recovered not from a lavish space that was used in the past but from an unexecuted design found among Daniel Burnham's plans for Field's in the early 1900s.

The fountain in particular is a testimony to the continuing "conversation" among the architects commissioned to design what was always intended to be Chicago's premier department store. It shows that what marks great architecture is both enduring beauty and its continuing influence over the passage of time. Marshall Field's State Street demonstrates these lessons, not only in the power of architects to build monumental buildings, but also in the ability of these buildings and their original plans to adapt to needs that were never imagined when the designs were first created.

The installation of escalators in 1933 was a sign that technology had acquired a level of style acceptable in this bastion of good taste and comfort. The escalator in the South Street main store carries a steady stream of patrons from floor to floor.

Christmas memories at Marshall Field's go back to 1887, when Harry Selfridge became the powerful general manager of the retail store. Selfridge was convinced that retailing was enhanced by great events and that Christmas at Marshall Field's should be the greatest

yearly event of all. Main floor decoration also has a timeless feel, as these photographs from 1938 (facing page) and 1940 (above) indicate. Windows and merchandise displays were often more topical.

Among the many unique selling spaces created in the State Street Store were several complete rooms from the great house of Whitehall in Shrewsbury, England, completed by the 1600s. In the 1920s, the paneling and other architectural details of the room provided an English setting for the Marshall Field furniture galleries. In the 1940s, some of the woodwork was moved to store president Hughston McBain's office (above). Today, it is stripped of whitewash and lines the board room in the eleventh floor offices of the State Street Store.

Photograph © Hedrich Blessing

By the 1980s, the retailing business was changing, and typical customers no longer preferred the cathedral-like emporium of old. Here at State Street, exclusive boutiques were what attracted the postmodern customer. Celebrity designers who created the shops changed the way menswear and many classes of goods were sold.

Marshall Field's attention to architecture has long made the store a natural setting for the most contemporary and fashionable home furnishings. In recent
years, the unveiling of the Trend House displays became a major event in design
circles in Chicago. While Daniel Burnham and his designers could not have
imagined what interiors would look like in 1989 (above) and 1990 (facing
page), the open space that characterizes the classic Chicago department store
lends itself to almost any configuration that the merchant could imagine or need.

In 1992, a new atrium rose 165 feet in space that had been an air-shaft between sections of the State Street Store. With a postmodern design, it brought a new touch of theatricality to an interior long known for jaw-dropping splendor. The fountain was cast from a design that was created long ago in Daniel Burnham's office but never executed.